Riri & Kiki

Volume 3

THE STORY OF BARBADOS AND THE SAILORS' VALENTINES

Written by: Sterlin L Blackman

B

Riri & Kiki

Volume 3

THE STORY OF BARBADOS AND THE SAILORS' VALENTINES

Written by Sterlin L. Blackman

Illustrated by Theresa Hynes, Palash Ghosh

ISBN:

Printed in the United States of America
First Printing, Gifts From The Ocean LLC

Acknowledgements

I would like to thank all those amazing people who encouraged, assisted, or contributed in any way to the production of the Riri & Kiki series and to this book in particular. Thank you, Douglas Blackburn, Susan Black, Sandi Blanda, Hatsue Iimuro, Alla Baksanskaya and the Barbados Museum and Historical Society. Thank you, Patricia Stafford, for going after the truth and dispelling the myths surrounding the identity of the Belgraves brothers. Thanks, and appreciation goes to all those who have played a part in keeping this art alive over the years.

Other books in this series:

- **Riri & Kiki Teach Pig Latin**
- **Riri & Kiki Teach Bajan Dialect**

The author seeks to give an accurate historical account of the Sailors' Valentines, however, neither the author nor the contributors of this book condone, encourage or support the killing of whales; we think it was a horrible act that should never be repeated. The world we live in has a very fragile eco-system that should be protected. All life is precious. Let this book be a deterrent of the wholesale slaughtering of any species.

Hi again. In this series of Riri and Kiki, we are going to explore the untold stories of our historic island.

Over the years, many stories have been told about the beauty of our island, Barbados. Although it is a small island in the Eastern Caribbean, Barbados' charm is very exhilarating and inviting. Our beaches are marvelous, and often people come to appreciate the beauty of nature. Furthermore, Barbadians are known to be very friendly and quite accommodating, as tourism does not only thrive because of the beauty of the island, but also the beauty that lies in the heart of our people.

Many tales have been told about our seas and our people; however, we have many more stories that have not yet been told about our beloved Barbados. Have you heard the story of The Barbados Land ship? Or maybe we can talk about cricket and the Great Excellent Sir Garfield Sobers, the greatest cricketer ever to grace a cricket field.

Furthermore, do you know the history of the Barbados chattel houses?

Let's not forget the story of Stede Bonnet, the gentleman pirate from Barbados, and his collaboration with Blackbeard. Or how about Sam Lords? Did you know he was a famous Barbadian buccaneer? There is also the story of 'King Jaja of Opobo and Becka, his Bajan sweetheart.

However, in this volume, we will tell the Story of Barbados and the Sailors' Valentines.

The story of the Sailors' Valentines is married to the story of whaling in the Caribbean.

From as early as the 1830s, Barbados got involved in the whaling industry. The local fishermen got involved in shore whaling; shore whaling is when the whales are spotted from land and a fleet of small boats, each carrying 6 to 9 men, set out to pursue and capture the whale.

The whale was then dragged into one of two ports: the beach at Holetown or the jetty at Speightstown, where they were flensed, and the blubber boiled.

While it is true that the British first landed in Holetown in 1625 to claim the island for the British, it was Speightstown that was the first major port and commercial center on the island.

Whaling was a large industry that involved whalers from around the world, including the British and American whalers. As the American whalers killed off local whales close to home, they were forced to travel further and further from home on voyages that lasted several months and even years. These large whaling ships would frequent Barbados' port for repairs, supplies, trading, and recruiting many native Barbadians as additional help on board the whaling ships because of death or desertion. Many ex-slaves welcomed this opportunity to escape from the plantation system and start a new life.

During their mating season, January – May, a large variety of whales would migrate from the cold water into the warm tropical waters of the Caribbean. In this so-called safe basin, they bred and gave birth to their calves. Of these varieties, the humpback and sperm whales were the most prized.

They were hunted for their oil, which was in high demand at that time. The sperm whales were hunted for Spermaceti oil, which is a valuable lubricant for watches and delicate instruments. They also got high-grade oil and a superior wax, which were used to make bright, burning, smokeless, as well as dripless, candles. This occurred during this period because the people made use of candles and oil lamps to see, since the electricity supply was in little or no use at all.

For these reasons, whaling had become a significant industry in the Caribbean. Barbados was already the most important port of call for the many ships trading in sugar, rum, fish and lumber. The large influx of whalers added to the number of sailors frequenting the island.

The city of Bridgetown itself festered with peddlers who had moved away from the hard labor of the sugar cane plantations. It was on the streets of the city that they peddled their craft; this included pottery, straw work, shell craft, fish, fruits and ground provisions to name just a few.

Of course, shell craft was not new to the region. Even before it became fashionable during the Victorian era, it was popular among the native Indians and the African slaves of the West Indies, who early on created a cottage industry out of the art.

The Yankee sailors, as the locals would refer to all whalers, were the big money spenders. On returning home after months, even years, at sea, the ships generally ported in Barbados to trade and do ship repairs. Some sailors took this opportunity to find the nearest pub, while for others, the purpose was entirely different. They came to shop for gifts to take back home for their loved ones.

Around 1833 Marcus Samuel, an English antique dealer, expanded his company to sell oriental seashells in London's East End. This new venture did so well that the company bought several ships and soon led the import/export market. The great demand for shells from the Far East also led Samuel to open several new outlets. One of these was the Shell Company, located in Bridgetown Barbados. This is the same shell company that would later merge with the Royal Dutch Petroleum Company and become one of the global giants in petroleum, while retaining the pecten as its logo.

Two other famous outlets that came in the latter half of the 19th century were the New Curiosity Shop on McGregor Street in Bridgetown and the West End Villa Museum located on Westbury Road in St. Michael. Both outlets were owned by the Belgrave brothers, B. H. and George Belgrave. The Belgraves were enterprising 'Free colored' who seized the opportunity to offer a central outlet for marine and nautical craft.

Thus, The New Curiosity Shop became one of the most popular shops visited by the sailors who were looking to buy souvenirs to take home, as a wide variety of nautical gifts could be purchased there.

The Victorian era had brought with it its new styles and fashions. Shell art, shell craft, and seashell jewelry were in great demand. The superstitious belief that wearing a seashell necklace around one's neck or displaying a piece of seashell ornament in one's home brought good luck also did much to help the industry prosper from as early as the first half of the 19th century.

The Curiosity Shop became the centralized outlet for the local craft and offered a wide variety of these souvenirs: seashells of all sorts and sizes, cured turtles, starfish, blowfish, flying fish, seahorses, shell chimes and a wide variety of seashell art and craft. However, before the opening of the curiosity shop and the Westend Museum, shell craft was peddled on the streets of Bridgetown

Industrious Barbadian women also seized the opportunity and made many of these gifts, including a type of octagonal shadow box with an intricately designed mosaic on the inside using local seashells. Originally called "Ladies Fancy Work," these Octagonal shadow boxes with visually appealing shell mosaics soon became a favorite of the sailors. These sentimental treasures proved to be the perfect token of love and friendship and were offered to their wives, mothers, sisters, and friends upon the seafarer's return from a long voyage at sea.

Barbados' large diverse shell population enabled this art to thrive. The craft evolved as it became more popular and personal, with the ladies engaging in customized orders. Many sailors began placing special customized orders while out on a trip, leaving photos of their loved ones or special messages to be crafted into the designs. Then, on their next visit to the island, they would collect the finished products to take home as gifts for their loved ones.

Eventually, overfishing had greatly depleted the humpback and sperm whale populations. This, along with the advent of kerosene, saw a reduction in the demand for whale oil. The whaling industry came to a halt at the turn of the 20th century, as many whale processing plants were forced to close. The large fishing fleets no longer visited the island of Barbados, and the large demand for such relics ended.

By the middle of the 20th century, The Myths of the Sailors' Valentines followed. In whaling ports of New England, New Bedford, Nantucket Island and along the continental east coast where the sailors most likely lived, these unique keepsakes started resurfacing with the term 'Sailors' Valentines' and many romantic stories behind them.

It was then assumed that sailors who were away at sea and missing their sweethearts, cherished friends and family, were the ones who created these beautiful and colorful tokens of affection while they were passing idle time on long sea voyages in order to bestow as gifts upon their return home.

However, it was later discovered that these beautiful shadow boxes were a part of the Barbados folk craft and were created by Barbadian women and sold to sailors who visited the island during the whaling era.

Soon after, on Nantucket Island and down the continental east coast from New Burry Port to Florida, seashell lovers started to reproduce these boxes on a more commercial level, adding more designs and offering some more modern versions while maintaining the theme of love and endearment.

A Gift From Barbados.
Photograph courtesy: Barbados Museum and Historical Society

NE WHALING
PORTS
NEWBURRYPORT
CAPE ANN
BOSTON
PLYMOUTH
CAPE COD
NEW BEDFORD
MARTHAS VINEYARD
NANTUCKET
N
W
E
S

On the island of Barbados, a strange thing occurred. For over three generations the art of Sailors' Valentines itself had ceased. It became a forgotten art in spite of the fact that relics were displayed at the Barbados Museum and several great houses around the island. It is strange because the locals continued through the years to produce other nautical crafts and gifts for sale to visitors to the island. However, the art itself was not revived until the 1970s and even then, it never got the type of engagement that was present in North America.

Maureen Edghill and Daphne Hunte are the two best known Barbadians shell artist. They both made a mark on the world stage with their exotic Sailor's Valentine creations. The revival of Sailors' Valentines on the island has not gained a great deal of attraction from the younger generation. However, of the few younger residents who dabble in the art, none stands out more than Douglas Blackburn, who has already received several local awards for his exhibits and a royal commendation signed by one of the Queen's ladies-in-waiting.

So, what are Sailors' Valentines? Sailors' Valentines are seashells glued in an octagonal wooden box covered in glass and sometimes attached in pairs. The original Sailors' Valentines are a form of shell craft. It consists of an eight-sided (octagonal) mahogany wooden box, 8" to 15" in diameter, displaying intricate, symmetrical designs composed entirely of small seashells of various colors glued onto a backing.

Patterns often feature a centerpiece such as a photograph, compass rose or a heart design, with phrases written in shells such as, "Forever yours," "Think of Me," "Home Again" or "A Present from Barbados." All of these are enclosed with protective glass.

Many Sailors' Valentines were made of two such boxes hinged together.

These were part of the collection of souvenirs or sentimental gifts made and sold in Barbados between 1830 and 1890 and designed to be brought home from a sailor's voyage at sea and given to the sailor's loved ones. Though the gifts were never given precisely on Valentine's Day, it is the extra mile that the sailors go that makes the gesture so appreciated by their loved ones.

The original Sailors' Valentines were composed of the octagonal shadow box with a sheet of Barbados newspaper glued to the bottom. On this was glued a layer of Sea Island cotton, to which the shells were then glued. The ladies exploited the natural color found in the large variety of small shells that were indigenous to the island. In some Valentines they even incorporated Crabeye seeds (Abrusprecatorius), which were also used in their jewelry making.

A Present From Barbados.
Photograph courtesy: Barbados Museum and Historical Society

Nevertheless, on account of the important part this concept plays in history, many artists have revisited the idea and have started trying to recreate the magic of the Sailors' Valentines in their unique way. They make it in such a way that the art is appreciated not just for the former beauty according to history, but also the beauty that the present ages bring. It is important to point out that even the contemporary arts are very exquisite and refreshing, as they are always made with the central theme of love and endearment, as they were originally.

So yes, the term "Sailor's Valentine" might not be a household name in Barbados today, but these beautiful shadow boxes originated here on this beautiful island and are probably one of the most significant reminders of the nostalgic whaling era.

Today there are still a handful of persons who are very passionate about the art of Sailors' Valentines. From the tiny island of its birth, this art has found its way around the world. This book highlights only a few of those passionate ones who have put great effort and time into researching, creating and teaching the shell art of Sailors' Valentines.

1. Douglas Blackburn -Barbados
2. Sterlin Blackman -Barbados
3. Susan Black - United States
4. Sandi Blanda- United States
5. Alla Baksanskaya – United States
6. Hatsue Iimuro - Japan

Turning shells into Art

Douglas Blackburn Shell Artist

Douglas Blackburn, law graduate of the University of the West Indies. In 2013 Douglas set out to do this new venture of shell art as a hobby, or so he thought. Six years later he was considered one of the leading shell artists in the Caribbean with several awards and a letter from Buckingham Palace complimenting his Art. This for the guy who thought he was not the artsy type.

Northern Star

The 25th Sailor's Valentine that I did was last Christmas's gift to my grandfather, Sydney Law, and in keeping with a design trend in some antique Valentines and some contemporary ones, I'd decided to put a photograph of my grandfather and I together in the middle.

When I gave it to Papa while we were all exchanging gifts, there were lots of tears in his eyes when he saw it and as I read out the card I wrote to accompany it "He is a giant among men, has been such an inspiration and guiding force to me, and we are all blessed to have him in our lives." My grandfather is great like the Northern Star in the Heavens to me, and he is the most important man in my life and has always loved and supported me in my work. I consider it an honor and a privilege to have made this for him, and to that end, I decided to name this piece "Northern Star". Now it hangs on a wall in a place of honor in my grandparents' house.

Northern Star

Douglas Blackburn

My Heart is Yours to Keep

This 18-inch box was my 8th Sailor's Valentine and the first one of this size that I'd ever done. Several antique pieces stood out to me where a unique design was employed with sets of double arches going around the box to create a circle, where, usually, a ring of shell flowers rested on a bed of silk, and that in turn encircled a central design. Sometimes the double arches were surrounded in turn by a border of spirulas or Rose Cups.

I used a combination of traditional shells that I'd collected locally, and some more contemporary ones used by shell artists today. I won't be listing them all because there are so many different species that I used, but I am most proud of the ring of flowers mounted en tremblant on the bed of pink silk. It was the most challenging part of the Valentine, and the very first time I did this traditional technique.

My Heart is Yours to Keep

Douglas Blackburn

Barbados – So Dear to My Heart

This particular Sailor's Valentine was the fourth and is an expression of my love for my country, Barbados, where (coincidentally) the art of Sailors' Valentines originated. I decided to keep with a traditional design and style, but by the same token, do something completely different than others have done; that something being to make a map of my country out of shells. I printed a map template, traced the design on the acid-free paper, lined it out with white rice shells, and then used different shells for each of the 11 parishes. For the surrounding ocean, I used blue mussel shells, which I crushed and fit together like a mosaic. For the other box, I did a simple design of an 8-pointed star with a traditional heart in the center.

For this Valentine, I used Ram's Horns, Rose Cups, Apple Blossoms, Emerald Nerites, Yellow Littorinas, Yellow Cowries, Red Pheasant shells, Blue Mussels, Coffee Bean Trivias, White Rice Shells, Purple Violet Clams, Mexican Green Limpets, Yellow Cowries, Violet Snails, Philippine Cup Shells, Black Littorinas, Red Limpets, Chiton Valves, Brown Snails, and lastly, the red and black seeds from the Crab's Eye vine.

Barbados
So Dear to My Heart

Douglas Blackburn

The Garden of Nereus

This particular Valentine was the 22nd I'd ever done and is currently my favorite piece. It won a Gold Award, along with another special award given out by the Barbados National Trust during NIFCA 2018.

I knew I wanted to make a really special, amazing piece with this one, and I also wanted it to have a very undersea theme to emphasize the ocean's rich and beautiful bounty. Some of the shells I'd been saving for a long time, waiting for the right moment to use them, and this was the right time. Everything was to be all-natural in this Valentine and the nautilus half in the centerpiece was the last of its kind, purchased from the Shell Gallery before it closed down for good.

The Garden of Nereus

Douglas Blackburn

STERLIN BLACKMAN

Growing up in the village of Connell Town, Barbados, Sterlin was introduced to shell craft around the age of eight, learning from the older boys how to make shell necklaces and bracelets. It was not long before he ventured away from mere seashell jewelry to broaden his inventory by producing picture frames and jewelry boxes, which became natural for him. However, it was not until 2007 that he tried his hands at creating Sailors' Valentines and became instantly addicted, "I do my own thing, experimenting with new styles, but I can also follow the original format as well."

I Love You

By

STERLIN BLACKMAN

Forever I do

By

STERLIN BLACKMAN

At One

By

STERLIN BLACKMAN

From the Garden of My Heart

By

STERLIN BLACKMAN

Tropical Gold

By

STERLIN BLACKMAN

The Greatest Love of All

By

STERLIN BLACKMAN

One Love

By

STERLIN BLACKMAN

Susan Black

Susan Black is the owner of Nantucket Sailors' Valentines. She was inspired to create this business while living on Nantucket Island. Her goal was to offer Sailors' Valentines in a kit form to make it easy to learn how to create your own Sailor's Valentine. Since then, her work has been published in various magazines and newspapers and has won awards for authenticity. Nantucket Sailors' Valentines was established in 2005. To view her kits and other related items, go to www.nantucketsailorsvalentines.com

Pink Rosette 2

Susan Black

Oceanscape-Cat Boat

Susan Black

Island-Memories

Susan Black

Special Occasion

Susan Black

Sandi Blanda

Sandi has been making Sailors' Valentines for over 36 years and has completed more than 600 pieces. She has done much research on the subject and has been offered the privilege to repair several original Valentines. She was one of those consulted and involved in the putting together John Fonda's amazing octagonal book on Sailors' Valentines. Besides having her work in several galleries and museums, she also found the time to teach this incredible art form starting in 2001.

Sandi Blanda

Sandi Blanda

Sandi Blanda

Sandi Blanda

Alla Baksanskaya

Alla Baksanskaya is an award-winning artist who works with natural seashells to make mosaic, mixed media paintings, Sailors' Valentines and sculptures out of beautiful, natural materials from all over the world. She combines the colors, textures and unique shape of each shell to make a truly exquisite piece of art. Alla finds beauty and simplicity in the uniqueness of seashells, corals, sea glass, driftwood, pebbles and pearls, using a type of this applied art called Coquillage. Alla's works are elegant, original and one-of-a-kind, since there are no identical shells in nature.

She won numerous awards at prestigious Sanibel Island, Florida, Philadelphia and New Jersey Seashell Shows from 2009 to 2020. She was introduced to and fascinated by the world of seashells as a child. Alla was born in Baku, Azerbaijan and spent so many summer vacations with her parents on a beautiful beach by the Caspian Sea. All her life is connected with the art. It is not just a career; it is a life passion. Since 1994, Alla has lived in NY with her family. It is where she has started to create art full time. Alla is the author of the book Seashell Picasso Nautical Mosaic: 18 Art Projects with 18 Hand Cut Templates and has developed 30 fun art and learning activities for kids called "Seashell Picasso Mosaic Kits." In 2015 Alla became a founder of The Art Fun Studio, a small business helping local kids and adults to make art with school trips and workshops and to celebrate their events with art.

Love

Traditional Single Sailor's Valentine, 2010, size is 11"x11." The shell mosaic includes geometric patterns, shell flowers and a sentimental message. In this Valentine are the list shells that were described in old antique octagonal shadow boxes, as referenced in John Fonda's book. This work was made for private order for the woman with first name is 'Love.'

"To My Sweetheart With Love Always."

Traditional Single Sailor's Valentine, size is 12 3/4" x 12 3/4". Third place, Yellow Ribbon Award in Sanibel, Florida Shell Show 2013, artistic professional category. This Valentine was made in an original antique octagonal box, using a strictly limited selection of seashells and Crab's eye seeds, which were described in John Fonda's book on the traditional Sailors' Valentines. The shell mosaic includes geometric patterns, shell flowers and a sentimental message.

"Happy 75th Shellabration!"

Contemporary Single Sailor's Valentine, size is 17"x 17." This is a very special King Neptune greeting for a 75th Sanibel Anniversary. The King of Neptune and his six horses were carved from the Jingle seashells in golden, orange, white and gray. Gar fish scales were used for eyes. For ocean waves in the mosaic tiny green Nerite Snail shells, Dentalium Weinkauffi vintage dyed-green shells and also crushed Spirula and Jingle white shells with tiny baby clam shells were used. In the center of the mosaic is Neptune driving a sea chariot, which is a Tridacna seashell and Junonia seashell with Allapora Pink coral, like a present for the Sanibel Jubilee. The beautiful sunny island Sanibel is made out of orange Jingle seashells and looks like a happy dolphin. The dolphin's eye is the seashell museum on the island, and on the nose is the harbor lighthouse. The complicated dolphin's eye is made out of two parts: A Gar fish scale and tiny Mussel "micro" natural, blue shell.

HAPPY
SHELLABRATION

"Ganesha"

Contemporary Single Sailor's Valentine, size is 11"x11." Third Place, Yellow Ribbon Award, 2011 New Jersey Cape Seashell Show. This work was made after an exotic and inspirational vacation in India, 2010. Lord Ganesha is a symbol of wisdom, wealth, success, and good luck in Hinduism. The center of the Sailor's Valentine is made out of Capiz seashells, along with a personal carving and painting done by the artist. In this work were used many different types of shells, as well as their fragments and Gar scales. All work was done with naturally colored seashells.

"Love Song"

Single Miniature Sailor's Valentine size: 5 ¾" x 1 ½" x 5 ¾". First place, Blue Ribbon, Best in the Show award in Sanibel 2013. This Valentine is made from tiny seashells with natural colors, sea urchins, their spines, and their fragments

Hatsue Iimuro

After a life-changing encounter with a Sailor's Valentine in Cape Cod, MA in 2005, her passion for shell art has led her to create lots of sailors' Valentines and even invent Japanese Sailors' Valentines, a new style of Sailors' Valentines merged with Japanese culture. Workshops have been held both in Japan and in the U.S. for her Sailors' Valentines admirers. In 2012, she became the first Japanese person to win the first prize in the Sanibel Shell show. She has won many other awards since.

Kai-Awase

"Blue Ribbon Award" and "Judges' Special Award" at Philadelphia Shell Show in 2012.

Kai-Awase, or shell matching, is a concentration-like game which was played among the aristocracy by pairing two parts of a clamshell. It was popular from the Japanese medieval period to the Edo period.

Normally, the inside of the clamshells is decorated with gorgeous "Kin-Paku" or "Maki-E."

"Kin-Paku," or gold leaf, is gold that has beaten to around 1/10,000 mm in thickness. It has been used in art, in architecture, and is now used for food or drink as a decoration.

"Maki-E," or sprinkled picture, is Japanese urushi lacquer sprinkled with gold or silver powder. The technique was developed in the Heian period (794-1185).

Hatsue Iimuro was inspired by that elegant culture of Japanese medieval nobilities to create this workSailors' Valentines in a contemporary style.

The inner side of the frame is covered with Tatami-Beri, the cloth used for binding the edge of tatami grass mats, giving it a very Japanese touch.

"Kai-Awase"

Floral Breeze

This 22″ walnut and maple Sailor's Valentine received a White Ribbon Award at Sanibel Shell Show in 2015.

This work has a scene of falling cherry blossoms cut out on it. Japanese people love not only the cherry blossoms in full bloom but also the whitish pink petals that leaveing its tree to flutter into the air. They find the scene so precious and beautiful.

Japanese traditional craftwork called "Koshu-Inden" is used with each edge of the octagonal frame.

"Koshu-Inden" is a tanned deerskin applied with Japanese urushi lacquer patterns, born in the 16th century in the Koshu region of Japan. They say that samurai warriors, wearing Koshu-Inden products, felt given power and protected by spirits.

Floral Breeze

Lighting Mirage 'Galaxy'

Red Ribbon Award at Philadelphia Shell Show in 2013

20' Walnut framed Valentine.

A transparent acrylic plate is used as a base of the frame with LED lighting installed, and translucent shells and opaque shells are effectively designed. The idea of using these two types of shells led to strong contrasts of light and shade on the work.

Hatsue Iimuro successfully invented a new Mirage by maximizing the effect of mirrors and light, which is capable of providing the reflection and expansion of the beautifully shining shells like stars in the galaxy.

Lighting Mirage 'Galaxy'

The beautiful sight of whales breaching and cruising along the coastline of the Caribbean islands is a wonder to behold. We are no longer blessed with large schools of these beautiful creatures migrating to our region, but there are still those who seek to rob us of this opportunity by hunting the few that survived the deadly assault. If history is forgotten, it is most likely to be repeated. Let the beautiful Sailors' Valentines of the whaling era not only allow us to revisit the glamour and creativity of the age, but be a warning of our fragile eco-system and a deterrent to those who would seek to rob our children of the experience of coexisting with these exquisite creatures.

WHALE SPECIES
BLUE WHALE
25M - 26.2M
SOUTHERN RIGHT WHALE
20M
SEI WHALE
16M
HUMPBACK WHALE
12.9M - 13.7M
FIN WHALE
20M
ANTARCTIC MINKE WHALE
7M - 9M
SPERM WHALE
16M
KILLER WHALE - ORCA
4.5M-10M

Made in the USA
Middletown, DE
25 February 2024

50285912R00046